Peace at the Last

Peace at the Last

Visitation with the Dying

Augsburg Fortress
Minneapolis

PEACE AT THE LAST
Visitation with the Dying

Cover design: Laurie Ingram
Interior design: Lorraine Klinger, Eileen Engebretson
Editor: Suzanne Burke

Manufactured in Canada.

ISBN 978-1-5064-1595-6

25 24 23 22 21 20 19 18 17   2 3 4 5 6 7 8 9 10

Introduction

Peace at the Last was birthed out of congregational need and experience in a specific time and place: Lake Chelan Lutheran Church in Chelan, Washington, beginning in 2007. A member said to me "Pastor, it feels like people are coming to us to die!" For a long stretch of time our little congregation was facing the deaths of so many. The last of our charter members were lingering at death's door. At the same time, several younger people—so vibrant and alive—faced chemotherapy and radiation, rising hopes dashed by the relentless diseases that afflicted the body.

Through this time of travail, the ministry of accompaniment was born. Our congregation has continued to be called upon to walk with people who are sick and facing death. People in our congregation and in our larger community have asked us to join them in their journey. Over the years, we have gathered a group of people who go to visit the dying, the sick, and the elderly. One of our people put it well when he said, "I'm completely afraid of being with people who are dying. So I know I have to go to them."

This honest expression of fear sparked a conversation about *why* people are afraid to visit nursing homes, hospitals, and sickbeds. What we found was that people are reluctant to go into such situations for fear of saying or doing the wrong thing. "Should I talk about death? Do I touch the person I am visiting? Should I pray? What do I pray?" These are all real issues for people who would like to bear witness to Jesus in the face of mortality, but who do not have what they need to do so.

From this came the idea of creating a liturgy for the visitation of the dying. Of course, pastors have prayers and liturgies at their disposal in pastoral care resources, but we wanted to create something that was accessible to *everyone* and that was visually beautiful.

For several months our group of eight or nine people met to gather resources that would be appropriate for such a liturgy. Our musician, Rolf Vegdahl, wrote several of the musical pieces in the liturgy. Others found or wrote prayers and blessings. We chose psalms by asking members of the congregation which ones they found most meaningful and reassuring. From start to finish, the liturgy is completely grounded in the experience of our congregation. We believe that truth rooted in a particular congregation can carry truth for the wider church. Indeed, isn't that what art itself makes clear?

While the liturgy was being compiled over 18 months, Wendy Schramm, the artist, was busy honing her watercolor craft. Lake Chelan Lutheran has a room dedicated to art and Wendy spent hours and hours in the art room and in the natural world around the Chelan area, painting and praying over the liturgy. When we finally had a complete draft of the liturgy, she went to work painting the frame for each piece. Restful and comforting beauty was her goal as she painted. What she found was that not every piece of the liturgy, and, of course, not every moment of dying, is restful. There are stark pieces in the liturgy that she has matched in visual art. Restful, stark, reassuring; it is all beautiful. And, as is proclaimed in the Akathist of Thanksgiving, "All true beauty draws the soul to You."

Beauty is at the heart of the Christian faith. We may discuss whether beauty is necessary or not, affordable or not, but as Alexander Schmemann points out, "Beauty is never 'necessary,' 'functional,' or 'useful.' And when, expecting someone whom we love, we put a beautiful tablecloth on the table and decorate it with candles and flowers, we do all this not out of necessity, but out of love." I would add that what the liturgy makes clear is that this beauty is an expression of *extravagant* love!

We who follow Jesus use this and all kinds of beauty to express the love of God to the least among us. It's a fool's errand in one sense—to create such a work of beauty for dying people. But I also believe this: if the church dedicated itself to just one thing, to accompanying the dying well, it would not be wrapped up in the anxiety of whether or not the church itself was going to survive. It would have no time for such anxiety. It would be too busy ministering to people who knew where to come to die and to live in the beauty of extravagant love.

—Paul Palumbo, pastor, Lake Chelan Lutheran, Chelan, Washington

About the art

It can be hard to visit the dying. When we decided to create this resource we wanted to make it easier. We wanted it to be read like a beloved children's book, a prayer book, or a hymnal. Creating the illustrations was my part of the project. Here in the rural Pacific Northwest we have few religious symbols. Living at the foot of the Cascade Mountains gives us daily opportunity to look at God's ever-changing creation. By using watercolor illustrations, many of them painted on location, I hoped to connect the sacred presence we see with the liturgical words and music we hear, speak, and sing.

When we use this liturgy, we begin in our church at the baptismal font. Our stained glass cross, and specifically the dove, visually continue throughout the pages. The pictorial memory of some of our favorite places connects word and sacrament to location and experience: looking down on the Chelan Valley from high on the hills, sitting in a boat on the still waters of Lake Chelan, hiking Railroad Creek Valley near Holden Village, and standing in the stark black of our burned forest. In these pages we also visually remember and share the touch of peace.

I pray that these illustrations, so meaningful to us, may be helpful to the larger body of Christ, and that others too may hold the comfort we have found in these pages.

—Wendy Schramm, artist

How to use this liturgy

We have included instruction on pages where explanations are needed. In addition, the following may be helpful.

1. Being present with the dying can seem like a daunting task. The first four pages of the liturgy are intended to give courage in the face of fears. Before going forth to visit, choose a centering space (church sanctuary, a home) to do the readings and prayers of preparation.

2. Be generous with silence, both in preparation and in the visitation. We have found that silence, often a source of anxiety in visiting, has become a time of richness and grounding. Make friends with silence.

3. The beginning of the visit should include warm greeting by name to the person facing death (whether they are conscious or not), and a kind touch on the shoulder. We often greet people with the kiss of peace.

4. The art and beauty of this work are for those who are visiting as well as for the person who is dying. It is appropriate to read or sing each page and then turn the book as one does when reading a picture book to a child.

5. When singing the chant "If We Live," take time to repeat as often as seems called for. "Mortal Days Are like the Grass" may be spoken or sung along with "If We Live." If sung, the music is found in the back of the book.

6. A number of psalms are included in this liturgy. We do not intend that all of them be used in a single visit. Choose one or more to be read or chanted. If a specific mood is discernible in the room, select a psalm that matches that mood.

7. Signing of the cross. An assigned person (visitor, family member) makes the sign of the cross on the parts of the dying person's body named in the liturgy. Take the index finger or thumb and mark the cross with a line top to bottom and left to right. This is a time for touch. In other words, it is not a sign of the cross *above* the body, but *on* the body. The sign of the cross is made as the blessing is voiced. Anointing oil may be used. After each signing, the refrain "Shepherd Me, O God" may be sung. After the last sign of the cross is made, those gathered may repeat the refrain several times.

8. A final song, prayer, and blessing conclude the liturgy.

May this resource bring encouragement and peace to you and to those to whom you minister.

—The Lake Chelan Lutheran Church Visitation Group
   December 2015

PREPARATION

We gather at the church before leaving for the visitation.

We are gathered in the name in which we are baptized:
In the name of the Father,
and of the ✝ Son,
and of the Holy Spirit.
Amen.

A reading from Isaiah.

But now thus says the LORD,
who created you, O Jacob,
who formed you, O Israel:
Do not fear, for I have redeemed you;
I have called you by name, you are mine.
When you pass through the waters, I will be with you;
and through the rivers, they shall not overwhelm you;
when you walk through fire you shall not be burned,
and the flame shall not consume you.
For I am the Holy One of Israel, your Savior.

Isaiah 43:1-3a

O God, you have called your servants
to ventures of which we cannot see the ending,
by paths as yet untrodden,
through perils unknown.
Give us faith to go out with good courage,
not knowing where we go,
but only that your hand is leading us
and your love supporting us;
through Jesus Christ our Lord. Amen.

Enter into the joy of Christ,
you servants of the Lord.
Do not fear death,
for the death of our Savior has set us free.

Participants may immerse their hands into the font and mark themselves with the sign of the cross.

MEDITATION

Rest silently.

GATHERING

Those accompanying enter the room of the visited. Sit close to the dying person.
Greet them. Offer the liturgy by beginning on this page.

We are gathered in the name in which we are baptized:
In the name of the Father,
and of the ✝ Son,
and of the Holy Spirit.
Amen.

COLLECT

Let us pray.
Holy and Living God,
by the mystery of the death of your Son,
you have filled the world with hope.
As we gather this day,
we draw near to his death and to our own,
remembering your promises
and trusting your Faithful One, Jesus Christ,
who lives and reigns with you and the Holy Spirit,
one God, now and forever.
Amen.

SONG

The refrain, "If We Live," is sung through twice and then hummed, as "Mortal days are like the grass" is read aloud by one reader. A musical version of the longer text, in the form of a descant, is printed on pages 59-61.

Rolf Vegdahl

If we live, we live to the Lord.   If we

die, we die to the Lord.   So then, wheth-er we live or

repeat as many times as necessary

wheth - er we die,   we   are   the Lord's.

24

Mortal days are like the grass.
They flourish like a flower in the field.
Wind passes over;
they are gone,
never to be seen again.

If we live, we live to the Lord.
If we die, we die to the Lord.
So then whether we live,
or whether we die,
we are the Lord's.

Everlasting to everlasting
is your love, O Lord;
your righteousness
for the children's children,
for your faithful ones.

Bless the Lord, O my soul,
and all that is within me.
Bless the Lord,
O my soul.
Bless God's holy name.

If we live, we live to the Lord.
If we die, we die to the Lord.
So then whether we live,
or whether we die,
we are the Lord's.

WORD

One or more of the following psalms may be read or sung on a simple tone.

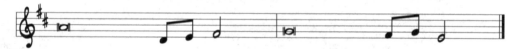

Psalm 23, page 30

For guidance and protection
Psalm 121, page 42
Psalm 139:1-17, page 46

For anxiety
Psalm 4, page 28
Psalm 46, page 35

For anger or bitterness
Psalm 39, page 32

For guilt
Psalm 51:1-12, page 36

For shame
Psalm 102:1-12, page 40

For rest
Psalm 131, page 45

Longing for death
Psalm 63:1-8, page 39

Psalm 4

[1]Answer me when I call, O God, defender | of my cause;

you set me free when I was in distress;
have mercy on me and | hear my prayer.

[2]"You mortals, how long will you dishon- | or my glory;

how long will you love illusions and seek | after lies?"

[3]Know that the LORD does wonders | for the faithful;

the LORD will hear me | when I call.

[4]Tremble, then, and | do not sin;

speak to your heart in silence up- | on your bed.

[5]Offer the appointed | sacrifices,

and put your trust | in the LORD.

[6]Many are saying, "Who will show us | any good?"

Let the light of your face shine upon | us, O LORD.

[7]You have put gladness | in my heart,

more than when grain and | wine abound.

[8]In peace, I will lie | down and sleep;

for you alone, O LORD, make me | rest secure.

Psalm 23

The Lord is my shepherd;
  I shall not want.
He maketh me to lie down in green pastures:
he leadeth me beside the still waters.
He restoreth my soul:
he leadeth me in the paths of righteousness
  for his name's sake.
Yea, though I walk through
the valley of the shadow of death,
  I will fear no evil:
  for thou art with me;
thy rod and thy staff they comfort me.
Thou preparest a table before me
  in the presence of mine enemies:
thou anointest my head with oil;
  my cup runneth over.
Surely goodness and mercy
  shall follow me all the days of my life:
and I will dwell in the
  house of the Lord for ever.

Psalm 39

[1]I said, "I will keep watch upon my ways,
so that I do not offend | with my tongue.

> I will put a muzzle on my mouth
> while the wicked are | in my presence."

[2]So I held my tongue | and said nothing;

> I refrained from rash words; but my pain be- | came unbearable.

[3]My heart was hot within me; while I pondered,
the fire burst | into flame;

> I spoke out | with my tongue:

[4]"LORD, let me know my end and the number | of my days,

> so that I may know how | short my life is.

[5]You have given me a mere handful of days,
and my lifetime is as nothing | in your sight;

> truly, even those who stand proudly are but a | puff of wind.

[6]We walk about like a shadow, and in vain we | are in turmoil;

> we heap up riches and cannot tell who will | gather them.

[7]So now, what | is my longing?

> O Lord, my hope | is in you.

[8]Deliver me from all | my transgressions

> and do not make me the taunt | of the fool.

[9]I fell silent and did not o- | pen my mouth,

> for surely it was | you that did it.

[10]Take your af- | fliction from me;

> I am worn down by the blows | of your hand.

¹¹With rebukes for sin you punish us;
like a moth you eat away | all we treasure;

    truly, everyone is but a | puff of wind.

¹²Hear my prayer, O Lord, and listen to my cry;
do not shut your ears to my weeping.

    For I am but a sojourner with you, a passing guest,
    as all my | forebears were.

¹³Turn your gaze from me, that I may | smile again,

    before I go my way and | am no more."

Psalm 46

[1]God is our ref- | uge and strength,

    a very present | help in trouble.

[2]Therefore we will not fear, though the | earth be moved,

    and though the mountains shake in the depths | of the sea;

[3]though its waters | rage and foam,

    and though the mountains tremble | with its tumult.

[4]There is a river whose streams make glad the cit- | y of God,

    the holy habitation of | the Most High.

[5]God is in the midst of the city; it shall | not be shaken;

    God shall help it at the | break of day.

[6]The nations rage, and the | kingdoms shake;

    God speaks, and the earth | melts away.

[7]The Lord of | hosts is with us;

    the God of Jacob | is our stronghold.

[8]Come now, regard the works | of the Lord,

    what desolations God has brought up- | on the earth;

[9]behold the one who makes war to cease in | all the world;

    who breaks the bow, and shatters the spear,
    and burns the | shields with fire.

[10]"Be still, then, and know that | I am God;

    I will be exalted among the nations; I will be exalted | in the earth."

[11]The Lord of | hosts is with us;

    the God of Jacob | is our stronghold.

Psalm 51:1-12

[1]Have mercy on me, O God, according to your | steadfast love;

　　in your great compassion blot out | my offenses.

[2]Wash me through and through | from my wickedness,

　　and cleanse me | from my sin.

[3]For I know | my offenses,

　　and my sin is ev- | er before me.

[4]Against you only have I sinned and done what is evil | in your sight;

　　so you are justified when you speak and right | in your judgment.

[5]Indeed, I was born | steeped in wickedness,

　　a sinner from my | mother's womb.

[6]Indeed, you delight in truth | deep within me,

　　and would have me know wisdom | deep within.

[7]Remove my sins with hyssop, and I | shall be clean;

　　wash me, and I shall be pur- | er than snow.

[8]Let me hear | joy and gladness;

　　that the body you have broken | may rejoice.

[9]Hide your face | from my sins,

　　and blot out | all my wickedness.

[10]Create in me a clean | heart, O God,

　　and renew a right spir- | it within me.

[11]Cast me not away | from your presence,

　　and take not your Holy Spir- | it from me.

[12]Restore to me the joy of | your salvation

　　and sustain me with your boun- | tiful Spirit.

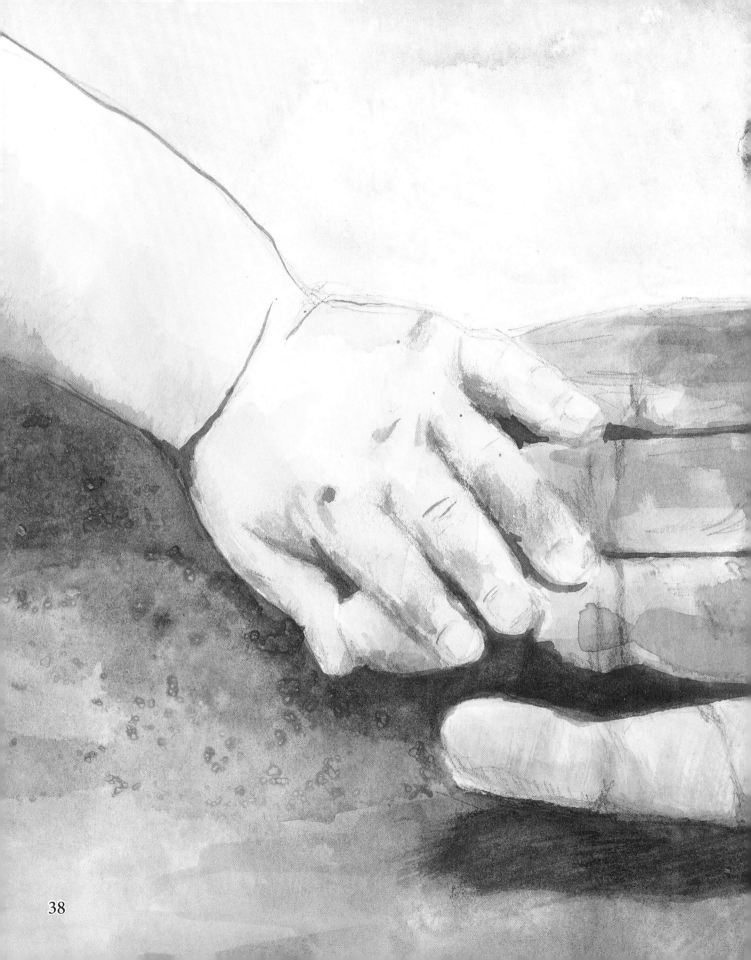

Psalm 63:1-8

¹O God, you are my God; eager- | ly I seek you;

 my soul thirsts for you, my flesh faints for you,
 as in a dry and weary land where there | is no water.

²Therefore I have gazed upon you in your | holy place,

 that I might behold your power | and your glory.

³For your steadfast love is better than | life itself;

 my lips shall | give you praise.

⁴So will I bless you as long | as I live

 and lift up my hands | in your name.

⁵My spirit is content, as with the rich- | est of foods,

 and my mouth praises you with | joyful lips,

⁶when I remember you up- | on my bed,

 and meditate on you in | the night watches.

⁷For you have | been my helper,

 and under the shadow of your wings I | will rejoice.

⁸My whole being | clings to you;

 your right hand | holds me fast.

Psalm 102:1-12

[1]Hear my ∣ prayer, O Lᴏʀᴅ,
　　and let my cry ∣ come before you.
[2]Hide not your face from me when I ∣ am in trouble.
　　Incline your ear to me; when I call, make haste to ∣ answer me,
[3]for my days drift a- ∣ way like smoke,
　　and my bones are hot as ∣ burning coals.
[4]My heart is stricken like ∣ grass and withered,
　　so that I forget to ∣ eat my bread.
[5]Because of the voice ∣ of my groaning
　　I am but ∣ skin and bones.
[6]I have become like a vulture ∣ in the wilderness,
　　like an owl a- ∣ mong the ruins.
[7]I lie a- ∣ wake and groan;
　　I am like a sparrow, lonely ∣ on a housetop.
[8]My enemies revile me ∣ all day long,
　　and those who scoff at me have taken an ∣ oath against me.
[9]For I have eaten ash- ∣ es for bread
　　and mingled my ∣ drink with weeping.
[10]Because of your indigna- ∣ tion and wrath
　　you have lifted me up and thrown ∣ me away.
[11]My days pass away ∣ like a shadow,
　　and I wither ∣ like the grass.

¹²But you, O Lord, en- | dure forever,
and your name from | age to age.

Psalm 121

[1]I lift up my eyes | to the hills;
    from where is my | help to come?
[2]My help comes | from the Lord,
    the maker of heav- | en and earth.
[3]The Lord will not let your | foot be moved
    nor will the one who watches over you | fall asleep.
[4]Behold, the keep- | er of Israel
    will neither slum- | ber nor sleep;
[5]the Lord watches | over you;
    the Lord is your shade at | your right hand;
[6]the sun will not strike | you by day,
    nor the | moon by night.
[7]The Lord will preserve you | from all evil
    and will | keep your life.
[8]The Lord will watch over your going out and your | coming in,
    from this time forth for- | evermore.

Psalm 131

[1]O Lord, I am not proud; I have no | haughty looks.

I do not occupy myself with great matters,
or with things that are too | hard for me.

[2]But I still my soul and make it quiet,
like a child upon its | mother's breast;

my soul is quiet- | ed within me.

[3]O Israel, wait up- | on the Lord,

from this time forth for- | evermore.

Psalm 139:1-17

[1]Lord, you have | searched me out;

O Lord, | you have known me.

[2]You know my sitting down and my | rising up;

you discern my thoughts | from afar.

[3]You trace my journeys and my | resting-places

and are acquainted with | all my ways.

[4]Indeed, there is not a word | on my lips,

but you, O Lord, know it | altogether.

[5]You encompass me, behind | and before,

and lay your | hand upon me.

[6]Such knowledge is too wonder- | ful for me;

it is so high that I cannot at- | tain to it.

[7]Where can I go then | from your Spirit?

Where can I flee | from your presence?

[8]If I climb up to heaven, | you are there;

if I make the grave my bed, you | are there also.

[9]If I take the wings | of the morning

and dwell in the uttermost parts | of the sea,

[10]even there your | hand will lead me

and your right hand | hold me fast.

[11]If I say, "Surely the darkness will | cover me,

and the light around me | turn to night,"

[12]darkness is not dark to you;
the night is as bright | as the day;

darkness and light to you are | both alike.

¹³For you yourself created my [|] inmost parts;
    you knit me together in my [|] mother's womb.

¹⁴I will thank you because I am mar- [|] velously made;
    your works are wonderful, and I [|] know it well.

¹⁵My body was not hid- [|] den from you,
    while I was being made in secret
    and woven in the depths [|] of the earth.

¹⁶Your eyes beheld my limbs, yet unfinished in the womb;
all of them were written [|] in your book;
    my days were fashioned before they [|] came to be.

¹⁷How deep I find your [|] thoughts, O God!
    How great is the [|] sum of them!

COMMUNION

Communion may be celebrated according to the traditions and circumstances of those gathered.

Gathered into one by the Holy Spirit, let us pray as Jesus taught us.

or

Our Father in heaven,
   hallowed be your name,
   your kingdom come,
   your will be done,
     on earth as in heaven.
Give us today our daily bread.
Forgive us our sins
   as we forgive those
     who sin against us.
Save us from the time of trial
   and deliver us from evil.
For the kingdom, the power,
   and the glory are yours,
   now and forever. Amen.

Our Father, who art in heaven,
   hallowed be thy name,
   thy kingdom come,
   thy will be done,
     on earth as it is in heaven.
Give us this day our daily bread;
and forgive us our trespasses,
   as we forgive those
     who trespass against us;
and lead us not into temptation,
   but deliver us from evil.
For thine is the kingdom,
   and the power, and the glory,
   forever and ever. Amen.

SENDING

The leader introduces this rite. One of those gathered may trace a cross on the body of the dying person as indicated while the leader speaks the words. Anointing oil may be used. Those gathered may respond by singing the refrain after each section.

Trusting in the holy and saving gospel
of our Lord Jesus Christ,
receive the sign of that gospel on your body
and in your heart.

Marty Haugen

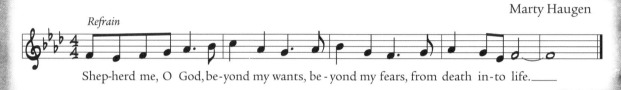

Refrain

Shep-herd me, O God, be-yond my wants, be-yond my fears, from death in-to life.____

Receive the ✝ cross on your forehead,
a sign of God's endless love and mercy for you.
Sing response

Receive the ✝ cross on your ears,
that you may hear the loving voice of Jesus
at your side. *Sing response*

Receive the ✝ cross on your eyes,
that you may see the glory of God face to face.
Sing response

Receive the ✝ cross on your lips,
that you sing praise to Christ with choirs of angels
and the whole host of heaven. *Sing response*

Receive the + cross on your heart,
that God may dwell there now and always. *Sing response*

Receive the + cross on your shoulders,
that you may lay down the yoke you have borne
and put your burdens to rest. *Sing response*

Receive the + cross on your hands,
that you may release this world and cling to Christ.
Sing response

Receive the + cross on your feet,
that you may dance in the company of the saints
forever. *Sing response*

Now, Lord, You Let Your Servant Go in Peace

Rolf Vegdahl

Now, Lord, you let your ser-vant go in peace: your word has been ful-

filled. My own eyes have seen the sal-va - tion which you've pre-

pared in the sight of ev-'ry peo - ple: a light to re-veal you to the

na - tions and the glo-ry of your peo - ple Is - ra - el._____ Now,

Lord, you let your ser-vant go in peace: your word has been ful - filled.

The Lord be with you.
And also with you.

Let us pray.
O Lord,
support us all the day long of this troubled life,
until the shadows lengthen
and the evening comes
and the busy world is hushed,
the fever of life is over,
and our work is done.
Then, in your mercy,
grant us a safe lodging,
and a holy rest,
and peace at the last.
Amen.

The Lord bless you and keep you.
The Lord's face shine on you with grace and mercy.
The Lord look upon you with favor and ✝ give you peace.
Amen.

MUSIC

If We Live

Rolf Vegdahl

Mortal Days Are like the Grass

Rolf Vegdahl

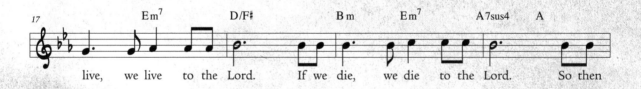

Now, Lord, You Let Your Servant Go in Peace

Rolf Vegdahl

Now, Lord, you let your ser-vant go in peace: your word has been ful -

filled. My own eyes have seen the sal - va - tion which you've pre -

pared in the sight of ev - 'ry peo - ple: a light to re - veal you to the

na - tions and the glo-ry of your peo - ple Is - ra - el._____ Now,

Lord, you let your ser-vant go in peace: your word has been ful - filled.

Acknowledgments

The Akathist of Thanksgiving is a prayer composed by Protopresbyter Gregory Petrov from a prison camp around 1940. Various English translations are available. The quote in the Introduction is from Kontakion 7 of the Akathist.

The Alexander Schmemann quote in the Introduction is from *For the Life of the World*, Crestwood, NY: St. Vladimir's Seminary Press, 1963, rev. 1973.

"O God, you have called your servants," "O Lord, support us all the day long," and the psalm tone music are from *Evangelical Lutheran Worship*, copyright © 2006, admin. Augsburg Fortress.

"Enter into the joy of Christ" is from *Benedictine Daily Prayer: A Short Breviary*, copyright © 2005 The Liturgical Press.

The text of "If We Live" is from Romans 14:8. Music is by Rolf Vegdahl, copyright © 2009 Augsburg Fortress. The text of "Mortal Days Are like the Grass" is adapted from Psalm 103. Music is by Rolf Vegdahl, copyright © 2016 Augsburg Fortress.

"Shepherd Me, O God," text (based on Psalm 23) and music are by Marty Haugen, copyright © GIA Publications, Inc. Used by permission.

"Receive the cross" is adapted from *Welcome to Christ*, copyright © 1997 Augsburg Fortress.

The texts of "Our Father in heaven" and "Now, Lord, you let your servant go in peace" were prepared by the English Language Liturgical Consultation (ELLC), published in *Praying Together* © 1988. Music is by Rolf Vegdahl, copyright © 2016 Augsburg Fortress.

ISBN: 978-1-5064-1595-6

51499